TERRORISM AS A FORM OF POLITICAL STRUGGLE

Ihor Halias

Lviv, Ukraine

2023

Annotation

This book explores terrorism as a complex and pressing phenomenon in the modern world, examining its history and its impact on political processes. The author meticulously analyzes the development and evolution of terrorism, paying attention to its methods, motivation, and ideology. The book also discusses the role and responsibilities of states in combating terrorism and proposes ways to overcome this threat to national and global security. The author shares their research and analysis, drawing on current data and statistics.

However, the book is not limited to theoretical aspects alone. It also examines specific examples of terrorist organizations from various parts of the world, their methods, and their consequences for society and politics.

Readers will have the opportunity to better understand the nature and mechanisms of terrorism in different contexts. This book will be a valuable source of information for anyone interested in the issue of terrorism and its impact on the contemporary political environment.

CONTENT

INTRODUCTION 4

CHAPTER 1. THEORETICAL FOUNDATIONS OF THE PHENOMENON OF POLITICAL TERRORISM 8

1.1 Concept of Terrorism and Fundamental Approaches to Its Classification 8

1.2 Subjects and Objectives of Political Terrorism ...27

CHAPTER 2. NATURE AND ORIGINS OF MODERN POLITICAL TERRORISM 38

2.1 State Terrorism as a Form of Violence................38

2.2 Nuclear terrorism is the greatest threat to humanity 60

CHAPTER 3. INTERNATIONAL TERRORISM AS A FORM OF POLITICAL TERRORISM 76

3.1 Preconditions for the Emergence of International Terrorism 76

3.2 Global Strategy to Combat International Terrorism 98

CONCLUSIONS 115

INTRODUCTION

Unfortunately, terrorism has become an integral part of global political and economic processes, escalating the threat to societal and national security. As a form of organized crime rooted in a powerful informal economy, terrorism can challenge the entire process of human development.

At this stage, humanity faces the threat of international terrorism. The term «international terrorism» has been used since the 1970s. The United Nations Code of Crimes against Humanity defines it as «the commission, organization, encouragement, or financing of acts by an agent or representative of one country to promote the interests of another state.»

International terrorism is also characterized by increasing ambitions and the scale of its objectives.

The events of September 11, 2001, served as a declarative challenge not only to the United States but also to the Western «golden billion» as a whole and the politics of globalization. This event, along with subsequent terrorist activities in other countries, led to certain consequences: mass panic, restrictions on civil rights and freedoms, and economic shocks. It can be said that international terrorism has become one of the forms of conducting war.

The relevance of this research topic is due to the need to study and generalize a series of important and complex events in international life related to politics and economics, which are of primary interest to contemporary terrorist organizations.

Furthermore, conflicts and tensions between states are also driven by issues related to national minorities, deported populations, refugees of terrorism – for which there are no borders – organized crime, drug trafficking, and money laundering.

For certain individuals, terrorist activities become a profession. Terrorists are well-trained and well-equipped, always operating against the clock, free from bureaucracy, and they always know exactly what they want.

Those facing a terrorist war must understand that it is a fight not just for survival but for life itself. From the terrorists' perspective, fear of death must be absolute, with no exceptions, including the elderly, women, and children. Understandably, terrorist warfare is a war of extermination, but it's a unique form of extermination. Terrorism is primarily a war to destroy human dignity, accomplished through the weapon of fear.

The scale of the terrorism epidemic and the force of its use can be determined based on statistical data and specialized publications from various state institutions worldwide. According to the «International Security Review,» there were 5,534 terrorist acts recorded from 1970 to 1978. In the year 1981, the «American Journal of Defense and Diplomacy» reported 2,700 terrorist attacks carried out by 125 terrorist groups operating primarily in 50 countries across the world. Data for the year 1985 shows a 15% increase in the number of these acts compared to 1981. According to the U.S. CIA, there were 6,714 international terrorist attacks between 1968 and 1980. In one of its annual reports, the CIA paints a striking picture of terrorism's spread, with terrorist attacks occurring in 48 countries in 1970, 57 in 1975, 76 in 1980, and 91 in 1981. By 1995, terrorism had spread to over 100 countries, and the number of terrorist attacks from 1968 to 1995 approached 25,000.

A memorial to the victims of terrorism was opened in Paris a few years ago. This fact, along with the recognition that in France, victims of terrorist attacks receive the same social status as war victims, naturally reflects the state's high level of attention, especially to its population. It's no wonder that this country is considered the cradle of democracy in Europe. However, these events are eloquent in a broader sense. Despite all the achievements of modern civilization, we are not only heroes of the struggle for freedom or pioneers in the field of science, but also victims of the actions of modern «bombers» who hold people's lives in their hands.

The chronological boundaries of this study are determined by its thematic focus and mainly encompass the 20th century. It was during this time that terrorism became a global issue for humanity, taking on new forms and employing new methods of subversive activity. However, at certain points, we step beyond these chronological limits to explain the causes of terrorism, understand its ideology, and grasp its essence.

CHAPTER 1. THEORETICAL FOUNDATIONS OF THE PHENOMENON OF POLITICAL TERRORISM

1.1 Concept of Terrorism and Fundamental Approaches to Its Classification

Throughout its historical existence, humanity has always sought to understand both itself and the surrounding world. In this regard, the legal realm is no exception. Humanity has long been interested in relationships, norms, and the nature and essence of rules that define their characteristics. Within the sphere of human understanding, terms such as «equality,» «freedom,» «justice,» and «law» shed light on the nature of law and its ontological foundations. These values hold significance and meaning in the life of individuals and society as a whole. In essence, the primary concern of the philosophy of law is the continuous search for the truth of law.

The present state of societal life demands philosophical and legal examination of the phenomenon of law in relation to the categories of freedom and morality. Therefore, the study of domestic and foreign literature and empirical data in the fields of legislation, governance, and jurisprudence should address the latest issues of political and information-legal reality.

The emergence and development of human rights are inseparably linked to the meaningful evolution of the principle of equality in different times and within various societal formations. The initial concept of the general equality of people emerged in ancient times, later developing in different forms and directions and achieving greater perfection in various historical periods. These developments found expression in legal behavior. As previously mentioned, its primary model was characterized by class restrictions. Consequently, these models were modernized, enriching their content and expanding it to include other social groups and countries.

In the development of human rights policy, our state has adopted norms developed in various United Nations and other respected international organizations' documents, which are accepted as a kind of standard for civil rights in the global community. Among the documents playing a crucial role in shaping our human rights policy is the Universal Declaration of Human Rights, adopted by the United Nations General Assembly in 1948.

The Declaration proclaims free and equal rights and dignity for all. It declares the inviolable right of all to life, liberty, and security of the person. It articulates both political and personal rights and forms part of the social and economic framework of the Universal Declaration of Human Rights, which was developed in the International Covenant on Economic, Social, and Cultural Rights and the International Covenant on Civil and Political Rights. Furthermore, the Declaration of the Rights of the Child was adopted in 1966.

The enactment of legal acts is the legislative recognition of all legally significant aspects of human freedom as a spiritual being, as a free, independent, and autonomous subject in all spheres of social life. It signifies the integration and protection of the individual and their will as the highest value.

Modern requirements concerning this issue are well reflected in the Constitution of Ukraine, adopted during the 5th session of the Verkhovna Rada of Ukraine on June 28, 1996. In the Constitution of Ukraine, it is stated that every person, their life, health, honor, and dignity, inviolability and security, are the highest social values. It is the fundamental duty of the state to promote and protect human rights and freedoms. Freedom of thought and speech are guaranteed to everyone (Article 34), and each person has the right to freedom of thought and choice of religion (Article 35). Ukrainian citizens enjoy the freedom to form political parties and public organizations for the protection of their rights and freedoms, as well as for the representation of their political, economic, social, and other interests that do not violate the rights and freedoms of others (Article 36).

The constitutional provisions (Article 28) on the protection of human dignity by the state have significant importance for the constitutional and legal integration of individual moral and religious, as well as general intellectual freedom and autonomy. Every individual has the right to liberty and inviolability (Article 29). The inviolability of a person's home (Article 30) and the confidentiality of communication, telephone conversations, telegraph, and other means of communication (Article 31) are guaranteed. These legal definitions, the integration, and the protection of personal freedom in the relevant areas of social life, such as personal and family secrets (Article 32), represent legitimate social norms and rules (morality, religion, ethics, aesthetics, etc.), as well as laws in the general system of social norms and social rules of this society.

Awareness and protection of human rights and freedoms today constitute a powerful element and a clear indicator of the progressive development of the global community based on the rule of law and its members for both domestic and foreign policy. As we know, a state is primarily a form of social organization, the main object of which is the human individual. The strength and power of any nation, particularly a lawful one, depend on its socio-political and legal maturity. Their existence is not only the subject of government orders but also the executor of the country's current laws, both those defined by law and those governed by universal moral norms, and they must be conscious subjects of their authority. In essence, they create the conditions for the existence of civil society and the further development of civil consciousness. This is an idea that has organically grown in connection with the idea of the rule of law.

At the same time, let us pay attention to some paradoxes of the concept of civil society. Its significance does not correspond to its name. In fact, civil society is not a civil society but a nation as a political phenomenon. In the field of civil society (contrary to its name), the subjects of public authority and public law are not citizens, but individuals with their interests, subjects of private law, and subjects of civil law.

Civil society is a voluntary society that constantly expands, connected to systems aimed at helping to reveal the inner potential of people and creating conditions for personal development and self-realization. It is predominantly achieved through association systems. Its activity is minimized and clearly defined.

In the process of formation and development of civil society, democratic and legal norms are established in all areas of social life, replacing old-fashioned and traditional methods of regulating human life. Civil society and the rule of law thus form a unity and represent a degree of democratization of political life and the political system as its institutional and legal mechanism.

Diversity of interests divides people into various groups, often with conflicting interests. Therefore, according to Hegel, civil society resembles a battlefield, where one's private interest is always incompatible with another's. Civil society cannot resolve these conflicts on its own. Only the nation can reconcile diverse interests. To achieve this, civil society forms a nation, creating a state structure and establishing legal relationships that define the procedures for their activities and cooperation. It is important to understand that individuals are not only entitled to exercise their rights and freedoms but also have a responsibility not to violate the rights of other citizens. This is formulated as «Freedom ends where the freedom of others begins.» Respecting the rights of others is the key to government law enforcement.

Government bodies (legislative, administrative, judicial) should assist civil society in creating and safeguarding optimal conditions for the uninterrupted functioning and resolution of conflicts. The nation, which serves civil society, represents the supremacy of the law. Civil society and the rule of law are interconnected. One cannot exist without the other.

The value, greatness, and purpose of human life in the universe require certain conditions for its vitality, primarily in accordance with the norms of spiritual law, the value of human life in society. It is undeniable that a person who violates the rights and freedoms of others commits a criminal offense. Civil society has certain categories of people who seek self-assertion and the achievement of specific goals (political, economic, social, ideological). People in this category achieve their goals through unlawful activities, including terrorism, but they must go through a series of transitional steps to achieve their desired outcomes. According to legislators, acts of terrorism cause the greatest harm to public safety, including the lives and health of people. Therefore, innocent individuals become victims of zealous fanatics who prioritize their ideologies. Terrorism involves violent acts or threats of violence aimed at intimidating, inciting, or obstructing actions in a direction opposed by the terrorists.

Over the past decade, one of the most dangerous new phenomena in the criminal situation in Ukraine has been the epidemic of organized crime. During this period, numerous organized criminal groups of all types have emerged in the areas of credit and finance, banking, foreign economic activities, illegal and semi-legal business, smuggling, drug trafficking, arms, and explosives trade, as well as terrorism.

Currently, a new dangerous phase is underway, where these groups are attempting to gain control over all aspects of small and medium-sized legal businesses, prostitution, and the entertainment industry. Fierce competition is ongoing, and these criminal organizations operate on an interregional and international scale, often having connections with mafia structures in multiple countries. The development of the drug trade is especially concerning, with Ukraine becoming involved in the global criminal system of drug production and distribution. The drug trade serves as a means of financing terrorist crimes.

Today, gangster trends are growing in many parts of the former Soviet Union. The attempt to forcibly achieve noble goals is a new and wild form of state terrorism. What's most terrifying is that this growth is gaining strength. Modern terrorists must realize that they are highly skilled professionals, not amateurs who used to throw homemade bombs into crowds. Until recently, terrorists typically used the latest advancements in military science and technology, including aircraft, satellite communication, and heat-seeking missiles.

In 1995 alone, Ukraine recorded approximately 240 terrorist crimes, including 164 involving explosives, 55 using grenade launchers, machine guns, and other weapons, 11 hostage takings, 14 agents of various levels captured, and eight police officers attacked. As a result of these actions, over 70 people were killed, and around 170 different buildings and 70 vehicles were destroyed or damaged. Law enforcement agencies seized dozens of firearms, ammunition, and explosive devices from the perpetrators.

International experience shows that terrorist activity can only be reduced through the concerted efforts of specially trained units by the state. Combating terrorism in our country is a top priority, and it cannot be addressed without the urgent establishment of a nation and a legal system to prevent and combat terrorism. To achieve this, based on the experience of countering terrorism in other countries, it is necessary to continue working on improving the existing legislation to increase accountability for the most dangerous crimes that threaten the authorities and the population.

In the fight against organized crime and terrorism, the implementation of internal measures is a multilateral international cooperation aimed at promoting interaction between law enforcement agencies and other national authorities in Ukraine and with foreign law enforcement agencies. There are more than 10 international agreements on combating terrorism, including the European Convention on the Suppression of Terrorism (1977), the Rome Convention on the Control of Unlawful Activities in the Area of Maritime Safety (1988), the International Convention against Taking of Hostages (1979), and others, which have assessed the same events at different times, with different and sometimes conflicting approaches, complicating the process of submitting applications, organizing, and liquidating cooperation between member states.

International experience in combating terrorism underscores the importance of creating mechanisms for implementing the provisions of the Convention by institutions performing police functions.

1) Determining their rights and responsibilities;

2) Developing cooperation between government bodies performing police functions in the fight against terrorism through INTERPOL.

3) Coordination of behavior between nations, especially among law enforcement agencies combating terrorism.

4) Regulation of legal aspects of cooperation, such as signing international agreements on various topics, including information exchange, joint operations at borders, tracking the location and movement of perpetrators of terrorist attacks, and control of weapons and explosives.

History shows that terrorism has been associated with humanity since ancient times when authority over people began to bring material benefits and became an individual dream without adhering to Christian commandments, morals, and the image of a person. In the 21st century, technological progress, the influx of some religious militants, and the struggle for power in the religious world as a whole have made this a «boundless» catastrophe. Technological advancements, means of transportation, and road networks have significantly improved the mobility of terrorists. By planting bombs in one state, criminals can be hundreds or even thousands of miles away from dangerous areas.

Therefore, new security threats are emerging worldwide, and this issue must be a top priority for contemporary international cooperation. These new threats should be understood as follows: terrorism, environmental degradation, invasion situations, HIV/AIDS, and other epidemics, international crime, illegal trade in arms and radioactive materials. Terrorism, much like drug trafficking, human rights violations, internal conflicts, uncontrolled migrations, refugee issues, poses a threat to human rights, the rule of law, democracy, and overall national and international security. Hence, these threats require enhanced research and analysis, as well as international determination and multilateral cooperation at all levels.

Terrorism is on the rise worldwide. In the 1980s, there were 500-800 terrorist attacks (in 1985), and in the 1990s, there were 900-1000 or more. According to criminologists, terrorists improve their activities every year, and terrorist acts become increasingly well-organized, involving explosives and modern weapons, causing harm to health and loss of life. In Russia, the number of terrorist attacks in 1996 increased 2.5 times compared to the previous two years.

Unfortunately, these terms are not reflected in Ukrainian legislation today, so we tend to believe that not everyone is familiar with them. Article 258 of the current Criminal Code of Ukraine defines the term «terrorist act,» which is far from what we want in the current criminal code. So, how can we talk about things we don't know? Finally, experts dealing with this issue have not yet reached a compromise on the precise terminology of this phenomenon. How should the general public react when they learn about terrorism primarily through the media?

So, what countermeasures can be discussed if society is not ready to answer this question, that is, if it is not ready to define what terrorism is? Given this, it is worthwhile to analyze the conclusions of researchers in this field and highlight their actual view of the current problem. In summary, the word «terrorism» is closely related to terms such as «white terrorism,» «red terrorism,» and «terrorist act.» An analysis of literature on this topic shows that there is currently no universally recognized definition of terrorism in the world. Although there are between 100 and 200 definitions of terrorism, scholars do not consider any of them classical.

Some writers may differentiate terrorism based on the nature of their behavior. Terrorism is an open and empirical act, while terrorism is carried out through conspiracy and unlawful conduct. Other authors often use these terms as synonyms. The author believes that a more precise definition is to say that terrorism is a crime, while terror is a method of action by any subject (state, organization, individual) using power, threats, and intimidation. First and foremost, the Russian explanatory dictionary by N.S. Ozhegov, edited by Shvedova, offers such an explanation of these concepts. Both this dictionary and the Ukrainian-Soviet Encyclopedia discuss the political orientation of terrorism. Polish scholar A. Bernard differentiates these concepts in his work «The Strategy of Terrorism.» Terrorism is violence and intimidation objectively used by the strong against the weak. Terrorism is violence and intimidation used by the weak against the strong.

A. Schmidt summarized this material and compiled a list of 109 definitions of terrorism in order to obtain a comprehensive definition of terrorism. After him, many researchers tried to do the same, but unsuccessfully; the new definition was even more confusing. One of the most important and long-lasting discussions regarding the concept of terrorism today is how to understand terrorism. That is, whether as national oppression or as non-state revolution. Terrorism is always associated with politics, as it pursues political goals and is based solely on political motivation. As Reagan once said in political debates about the contrast in Nicaragua, we see that «terrorists can easily become freedom fighters.» Governments of some countries label armed struggles of political opposition groups as terrorism, justifying the latter by trying to prove that the state is using «terrorism tactics» against them.

A similarly complex aspect of this definition is understanding terrorism as a form of war or as a form of violence. Unlike the military, terrorists do not attempt to conceal their criminal intentions, do not have specific territory where combat operations take place, lack neutral territory, and have no restrictions on specific types of weapons. The military recognizes that using weapons against civilians is an exception or a misunderstanding, while terrorists have the opposite goal, and their aim is to instill fear, panic, and terror in people, primarily targeting civilians worldwide. Wilkinson says that it is actually very difficult to draw the line between war and terrorism. However, this fact does not turn every guerrilla war that deviates from the rules of war into terrorism. Therefore, it is advisable to distinguish these terms. They should never be generalized.

In general, the analysis of existing scientific views on the nature and characteristics of this phenomenon, as well as international legal documents and the current criminal legal content of a number of countries, including Ukraine, define the following characteristics of terrorism as recognized by societies:

- The use of organized violence that threatens the lives and health of people.

- Deliberately creating an atmosphere of terror.

- Mass shock that disrupts the operation of economic or organizational entities.

- Public nature of terrorist acts.

- Someone always takes responsibility for terrorist acts.

- Infliction of harm directly to third parties to achieve the goal.

- An increase in social danger.

Therefore, terrorism in the form in which it is practiced poses a threat to people through violence. It encompasses physical, political, social, economic, informational, and other forms of violence. If there are many specific forms of violence, the most productive at this stage are complex forms based on at least two parameters: the level of violence and the level of organization. Overlaying these two indicators allows us to distinguish four main types of violence: group organization and group volunteers, individual volunteering, and individual organization. It is clear that each of them has its own characteristics that are inherent only to that specific type.

The main problem facing humanity is the dual assessment of historically created terrorism. This narrow and practical logic prompts everyone to distance themselves from each other after the notorious «double standard» in assessing terrorism. In reality, there is no such thing as «good» and «bad,» «useful» and «harmful» terrorism. These are merely our subjective assessments that cloud our understanding of reality. Terrorism is, in fact, a product of a combination of specific conditions in society, which may seem to create the impression of a politically neutral tool used by a certain group to achieve their declared ideal. Essentially, it is a set of violent methods designed to achieve these goals through any means and at any cost. The characteristics of terrorism stem from who uses it, who controls it, and who evaluates it from the perspective of convenience or harm in achieving the ultimate result.

Therefore, the following definition of terrorism can be proposed by summarizing the sources and scientific developments of domestic and foreign researchers on this issue. Terrorism is a social, legal, political, and economic instability in a country with the aim of making certain changes (compliance with conditions) in favor of criminals through the threat of force or the use of weapons. It is a social phenomenon that is created and exacerbated. Explosions, arson, and other acts of public endangerment by a specific individual or group of organized individuals, resulting in harm to people, constitute terrorism.

1.2 Subjects and Objectives of Political Terrorism

In contemporary literature, there are more than 100 definitions of the concept of «terrorism.» However, all researchers agree that terrorism is a particular form of violence against innocent people. Prominent terrorism researcher B. Jenkins (USA) believes that a violent campaign that generates a threat of violence, individual violence, or fear can be defined as terrorism. Armed violence without a clear front line, not limited by geographical borders or norms, and secrecy in operation preparation and their unsystematic nature—all of this has led to «terrorism advocates» like B. Jenkins being transformed into a new type of political organization. It is clear that war and terrorism cannot be equated, but they are closely related, and sometimes intertwined, as evidenced, for example, by events in Chechnya.

British researcher P. Wilkins writes that terrorism fundamentally differs from other forms of violence not only in its brutality but also in its higher amorality, lack of understanding of means, and uncontrolled nature. Sovereign Ukraine shares a deep concern of the

European and global community about the epidemic of international crime and terrorism, and it seeks to use international legal expertise to combat these dangerous legal phenomena. We aspire to become a civilized state governed by the rule of law. This is associated with the unpredictability of the outcome, a high number of casualties after a terrorist act, and a relatively high effectiveness in achieving terrorist goals.

International terrorism is a crime, the common goal of which is international relations. Terrorism is defined as an act of violence or a threat of violence aimed at incitement or obstruction of acts in the desired direction for terrorists. A terrorist act is always an act of violence and aggression and has the following characteristics:

- Various forms of violence, making it the most effective choice for attracting public attention.

- The terrorist act itself is directed against an individual or group of people.

- The absence of a real possibility to achieve goals without resorting to violence.

When international relations are compromised, international terrorism should be viewed as a multi-level crime that affects:

- The functions of the diplomatic system.

- Ensuring national sovereignty.

- Ensuring the right to ethnic self-determination.

- Ensuring the special legal personality of international intergovernmental organizations.

- Ensuring human rights and freedoms.

- The usual function of international land, air, and maritime communications.

The main sectoral goals of terrorism are:

- National sovereignty.

- The diplomatic system.

- International land, air, and maritime communication systems.

The issue of classification and qualification of terrorist acts is resolved based on an analysis of the differences in the subject of implementation and the target orientation, taking into account the degree of threat to international relations. The decisive factor in recognizing an act of terror as a crime against nations is its composition and the relationship between crimes against peace, crimes against humanity, genocide, apartheid, and other crimes against nations. Regarding terrorist acts falling under international law, the following conclusions can be made:

1) Terrorist attacks can occur in both peacetime and wartime.

2) It is necessary to distinguish terrorist acts by the subject of the action and by the subject of orientation: by the subject of action, terrorist acts committed by individuals who are ordinary and specially prepared for this purpose.

Terrorist acts are classified into the following categories:

- Terrorist attacks on national security.

- Terrorist attacks on people.

- Terrorist attacks on national, individual, or corporate property.

3) Terrorist attacks fall under the purview of international law for the following reasons:

- Its mission from international law.

- Threat to international affairs.

- The presence of international elements.

- National interests versus the social danger posed by certain types of terrorism.

The international element means that a terrorist attack extends to:

- The territory of one or more states or territories not belonging to any of these jurisdictions.

- The property of foreigners or foreign individuals or legal entities.

Therefore, terrorist attacks should be understood as acts of violence against individual persons, groups of people, classes, officials, and nations with the aim of achieving, threatening, or inciting the fundamental goals of a terrorist attack.

Terrorism, as a sociopathic phenomenon, has been a violent means of seizing and maintaining power for centuries. The generalization of global experience shows that terrorist activity can take the form of both domestic and international terrorism. During the 19th century, terrorism remained primarily an internal phenomenon. In the 20th century, international terrorism reached incredible activity. Domestic terrorism occurs within the territory of a state. Terrorists and victims are citizens of that state. International terrorism is carried out by terrorists against foreign citizens, representatives of international organizations, and foreign citizens whose citizens are on the territory of a non-terrorist country.

Terrorism manifests itself directly in the form of committing terrorist acts, which constitute the commission of terrorist crimes, which are the final stages of terrorist acts. Terrorist activities are often prolonged and involve the preparation and execution of terrorist acts. Combat groups, reconnaissance groups, material-technical support, security, and safety may be involved in the operation. A terrorist group is a subject of a terrorist organization whose duties include activities directly related to the preparation and commission of terrorist acts. Terrorist groups consist of terrorists directly involved in terrorist activities and are characterized by close cooperation among their members to achieve specific goals. Terrorist activity is characterized by the number of classes, relatively long duration, the existence of hierarchies, the division of administrative functions, and the conduct of terrorist acts, intelligence, public relations, and financing. In different regions of the country and in some countries, there may be branches of such terrorist groups.

After the collapse of the Soviet Union, a number of conditions emerged on its territory for social, national, idealistic, psychological, and pagan tension. First and foremost, the collapse of the integral system, paralysis of power, and a protracted economic crisis, a sharp decline in the living standards of the majority of the population and their subsequent poverty, exacerbation of social contradictions, and a change in worldviews led to a decrease in the level of morality.

The prolonged war in Afghanistan became a kind of training ground for members of terrorist organizations. Given its brutality, impossibility of achieving victory, and other negative factors, it became a habit to break the spirit of thousands of compatriots, resorting to anger and brute force in the fight against the enemy.

Terrorism in the former Soviet Union countries is similar in its contours to the well-known terrorism with all its symptoms. This is evidenced by the explosion in Vladikavkaz in 2003 at the central market. Terrorists planted explosive devices among the rows of vegetables, which were always crowded. According to experts' estimates, its capacity was equivalent to 7 kg of TNT.

Over 200 people were injured, 62 of them died. Negative phenomena and processes that pose a real threat to our country are taking place in our society: socio-economic crisis, political conflicts, strengthening of separatism, poverty, and very low concentration of the majority of the population, crime, business and corporate integration, state corruption, organized crime, massive illegal arms trade, moral and spiritual decline.

Statistics indicate that Ukraine is increasingly facing a trend of terrorist crimes involving homemade explosive devices. In the period from 2003 to 2004, more than 560 crimes were committed in Ukraine, resulting in 90 fatalities (including 15 government officials) and 218 injuries. Analysis shows that these actions generally have a criminal component in the distribution of influence in illegal entrepreneurial activities aimed at eliminating competitors and in the fight with the intention of killing or intimidating government officials.

Today, a serious problem is the illegal trade in all types of weapons and military equipment, ammunition, explosive substances, technology with defense and dual-use purposes, specific raw materials, and materials used in the development or production of weapons, military, and special equipment. This poses a real threat to international stability and security. Its import and export are controlled in accordance with international agreements.

International experience shows that terrorist activity can only be reduced through the concerted efforts of specially trained units by the state. Combating terrorism in Ukraine is a priority and cannot be resolved without the urgent establishment of a state-legal system for preventing and countering terrorism. To achieve this goal, relying on the experience of counter-terrorism in other countries, we will increase responsibility for the most dangerous crimes to exert pressure on government institutions and the public, and continue efforts to improve existing legislation. Domestic actions, combined with multilateral international cooperation, should contribute to cooperation between law enforcement agencies and other government bodies in Ukraine in the fight against organized crime, terrorism, drug trafficking, and more.

There are more than 10 international anti-terrorism agreements, including the European Convention on the

Suppression of Terrorism (1977), the Rome Convention for the Suppression of Unlawful Acts against the Safety of Maritime Navigation (1988), the Taking of Hostages Convention (1979), issued at different times and with different, sometimes opposite approaches and assessments of the same event, complicating the procedure for its application and ensuring proper organization of cooperation among participants, which makes its implementation challenging.

Ukrainian researchers, such as V. Yemelyanov, V. Glushkov, Y. Kondratyev, V. Lipkan, and others, are currently developing and adopting a unified international treaty on combating terrorism within the international community. Taking into account international human rights experience, terms like terrorism and terrorist acts have been defined, clear procedures for cooperation between states have been established, conditions for the forced extradition of terrorists to affected countries have been provided, and the terrorist policy pursued by the state, as pursued by the country's government bodies, has been outlined.

International experience in combating terrorism underscores the importance of creating a mechanism for implementing the provisions of the convention by law enforcement agencies. This mechanism includes:

- Defining the rights and responsibilities of institutions performing policing functions.

- Facilitating cooperation between government authorities responsible for policing functions in the fight against terrorism through Interpol.

- Coordinating behavior among nations, especially among law enforcement agencies combating terrorism.

- Addressing legal aspects of cooperation, such as signing international agreements on various topics, including information exchange, joint practical actions at borders, tracking the whereabouts and movements of terrorist attack perpetrators, and control over weaponry and explosives.

Regarding examples of public terrorism, methods of terror that target peaceful, defenseless individuals who have no connection to the «recipient» of the attack are becoming increasingly effective and impactful. Moreover, organizers of such attacks ensure that the catastrophic consequences of their actions are prominently displayed in the media.

CHAPTER 2. NATURE AND ORIGINS OF MODERN POLITICAL TERRORISM

2.1 State Terrorism as a Form of Violence

Intentional and Deliberate Hostage Taking, Arson, Killings, Torture, Threats to Civilians and Authorities, or Other Interference with the Lives and Health of Innocent People, or the Threat of Committing Criminal Acts with the Aim of Exerting Control over the Political Situation in Society.

The definition of the term «terrorism» is a problematic issue as there are currently over 100 definitions of this phenomenon. However, none of them has gained wide recognition in the international community. Ukrainian lawyers V. Yemelyanov and S. Havrysh explain that in the framework of Ukrainian legislation, terrorism is considered by modern science in three aspects: criminal activity, terrorist groups (organizations), and the terrorist doctrine. V. Lipkan views terrorism as a negative socio-legal phenomenon and doesn't limit it solely to acts of explosions and arson but also encompasses actions falling under the term «terrorist act.» Terror is the fear, the fear of policies that pose a threat of terrorism, and the coercive repression of political opponents. O. Kostenko believes that it is possible to formulate a universal concept of terrorism. For this purpose, he defines terrorism as a «conscious threat to the people's will.» Therefore, terror is the use of terrorism, the deliberate creation of threats to influence the will of the people.

It is necessary to distinguish three related but substantially different concepts of terrorism: terrorism, terror, and national terrorism. Terrorism is violence by the government and its national institutions against the people with the aim of suppressing not only opposition but also the general public, causing terrorism, and renouncing the idea of resistance. In other words, terrorism is violence by those in power. Systematic political terror was first revealed by the Jacobins during the French Revolution. Their immediate ideological descendants were the Bolsheviks, who unleashed the «Red Terror» to subdue political opposition and spread Bolshevik rule beyond the captured cities of Petrograd and Moscow. It is estimated that the victims of terrorism numbered in the hundreds of thousands and even millions.

French historian Auguste Cochin, a renowned researcher of the French Revolution, concluded that democracy is the rule of «ordinary people,» and terrorism is an inevitable attribute of democracy. Due to the fundamental democratic dichotomy between the reality of political relations and fantasy, those in power intentionally shape public opinion with the support of various entities, initially in France through Masonic lodges and later through political parties. To correct the failure of this system, extreme measures, such as terrorism, are the only recourse to maintain the ruling minority in power. This is evidenced by the political history of 19th-century France. Ukrainian scholar Igor Shafarevich arrived at a similar conclusion about terrorism while studying the consequences of the Russian Revolution of 1917.

On the other hand, terrorism is a form of «weak» violence that often emanates from societal opposition, sometimes radical, and generally lacks support from democratic societies. Terrorism can have political, social, national, or religious characteristics. As a phenomenon, it typically has at least three primary and significant objectives. First, it exerts pressure on those in power to intimidate them. Second, it creates fear and unease among citizens who pledge allegiance to existing higher authorities. The third objective is to garner sympathy for their potential supporters, individuals who view those in power as repressive or discriminatory but less radical than the terrorists.

Terrorism can also be employed by specific factions within the dominant minority to seize full control of power.

State terrorism is state-sponsored violence without legal or judicial support, which can be carried out by national law enforcement agencies either domestically (against internal enemies) or abroad, including special operations against other states. Unlike international terrorism (when used within a country) and war (when used against other states), the involvement of state security forces in state terrorism is carefully concealed.

Terrorism, as a phenomenon, is driven by social, political, and economic factors. The most comprehensive attributes of terrorist activities were outlined by Bruce Hoffman in his book «Inside Terrorism.»

Indicators of such activity include:

- Exclusively political motivation.

- Violence or the threat of violence.

- Intended for long-term psychological consequences, as well as the destruction of specific victims and objects.

- Carried out by an organization with a recognizable set of commands or clandestine structures of focal points, whose representatives do not wear uniforms or distinguishing signs.

In his book «Terrorism and Political Violence: Understanding Them,» Dipak K. Gupta analyzes several situations that are typically considered conducive to the emergence of terrorist movements in a state:

1) Poverty. It may seem challenging to assert, but there is an obvious connection between national poverty and terrorism. However, when looking at the members of terrorist organizations, one can see that terrorists belonging to the poorest strata of the population are generally representatives of the middle class. Moreover, sociological research in the Islamic world shows that individual poverty among citizens has a very weak correlation with support for terrorist groups. Viewing

poverty as a societal rather than an individual problem, 20-40% of the population lives below the poverty line, with the lowest being 80%, and most deaths from terrorist attacks occurring in these countries. Thus, despite the common belief that human poverty is directly proportional to the potential of terrorist organizations, this correlation is weak at best.

2) Lack of democratic freedom. After the September 11 attacks, George W. Bush's administration quickly found an explanation for the actions of terrorists: «They hate our freedom.» However, if one does not view terrorism solely as religious radicalism, it becomes evident that in democratic Britain and Spain, «homegrown» terrorists like the IRA and ETA cannot defeat «foreign» radicals like Al-Qaeda. The difference lies only in what they are fighting for—freedom for some and what a group of people has devised for others. If totalitarian or authoritarian regimes are examined, the number of terrorist organizations there is very low (countries like Cuba, China, and the Soviet Union). Meanwhile, countries with «suspicious democracies» suffer from terrorism. These countries, like Russia, Pakistan, and Iraq, where the state imparts only part of

the «set» of democratic values to its citizens. Therefore, the absolute absence of democratic freedom is not a determining factor for the formation of terrorist organizations in society.

3) Weak central authority (often separatism). Government impotence here implies not only the «entanglement» of the state in «anarchy» or the government's inability to formulate a clear policy but also the existence of large territories beyond the control of the central government. The connection with the emergence of terrorist organizations is most evident here. The balance between costs and benefits sharply declines due to the expansion of opportunities for terrorist organizations (centers in remote, uncontrollable areas) since the government cannot establish clear control and rapid response on the ground.

4) Struggle for power. This is mainly a desire for absolute power. Potential terrorism (primarily the assassination of politicians) by representatives of the so-called middle class precedes almost every social (bourgeois) revolution.

Terrorism is criminally defined as the use, intimidation, application of violence, or commission of other dangerous actions, undertaken by a state, international organization, physical or legal person, or group of people with the aim of destabilization, intimidation, or oppression.

Ukrainian scholars, including V. Yemelyanov, generally define terrorism as a dangerous act or threat that disrupts public opinion, violates social security, and creates an atmosphere of fear, anxiety, and depression directly in the social arena.

State anti-terrorism laws identify specific types of killings that can be considered indicators of terrorism, including poisoning, electromagnetic means, weapons of mass destruction (bacteria, chemical substances, nuclear weapons), and explosions targeting innocent individuals.

Terrorist acts, such as killings, injuries, abductions, intimidation, and other acts of violence, are planned by organizations and carried out by individuals against politicians and officials, accompanied by achievements of modern society. History has witnessed many international acts of terrorism, including the assassinations of Abraham Lincoln and John F. Kennedy, the 16th and 35th Presidents of the United

States, Prime Minister of India Rajiv Gandhi, and Prime Minister of Israel Yitzhak Rabin.

All of these terrorist acts, regardless of their mission's motives, were common crimes and were prosecuted according to the laws of the country in which they occurred. International terrorism of today has significantly expanded its borders. In essence, terrorism that affects the interests of two or more states and violates international law.

International terrorism is a special form of terrorism that began in the late 1960s and grew significantly at the end of the 20th and the beginning of the 21st century. Its main objectives today include administrative disruptions, economic and political missions, and the violation of the very foundations of social institutions, which, according to terrorists, should compel governments to change their policies. There is no universally accepted definition of international terrorism. In practice, this term is often used as a political tool, as each country decides whether a group belongs to the category of «terrorists» or «freedom fighters,» and terrorist acts occur locally.

The main characteristics of international terrorism are globalization, specialization, and reliance on extremist idealism. There are also threats related to the use of suicide terrorists, unconventional (nuclear, chemical, biological) weapons, and rational approaches. Brian Jenkins, one of the modern researchers of terrorists, views international terrorism as a new form of conflict.

UN Security Council Resolution 1373 of September 28, 2001, states: «International terrorism and transnational organized crime, illegal drugs, money laundering, illegal arms trafficking, as well as nuclear, chemical, biological, and other potential. It is closely related to the illegal trade in hazardous substances.» Experts also note the increasing technical capabilities of terrorists and implicit support from certain states.

Terrorist organizations extensively utilize the internet, radio, and television to achieve their goals.

International terrorism is particularly dangerous because it threatens international law and interstate relations.

Terrorist acts can be classified as international crimes if:

- The terrorists and the victims of the attacks are citizens of different states, but the crimes are committed outside these states.

- Terrorist acts are directed against individuals receiving international protection.

- Preparation for terrorist acts is carried out in one country and on the territory of another.

- After committing a terrorist act in one country, the perpetrator hides in another, making it difficult to bring them to justice.

Encyclopedic dictionaries, especially legal ones, define the concept of terrorism from an international perspective.

International terrorism is a violent crime that has international consequences, typically aimed at intimidating or causing harm to individuals or society for political purposes. It also includes violence against specific citizens or entities protected by international law. This encompasses the killing of foreign heads of state and governments under international law, the dissolution of embassies and diplomatic missions, attacks on international organizations, public places, roads, airports, stations, and more.

Terrorism involves the abduction, kidnapping, killing, or endangering innocent people, as well as critical economic assets, life support systems, communication, the use of nuclear weapons, or the threat of their use (nuclear terrorism), chemical weapons, biological weapons, and other forms of mass destruction or the threat of using them.

Political, economic, and criminal terrorism find common ground based on mutual interests.

Today, there are several types of terrorism:

1) National-liberation terrorism: This is sometimes referred to as terrorism of ethnic minorities. The main demand is liberation from oppression or complete state autonomy to eliminate discrimination and oppression. Examples include the Northern Ireland, Catalonia, Basque, Breton, Corsican, South Tyrolean German, Franco-Canadian, Kurdish conflicts, etc. The existence of such terrorism (partially reconciled after voluntary demands by Catalans, South Tyrolean Germans, Franco-Canadians, and some Corsicans) was a matter of oppressed nations and ethnic minorities, and modernization in the mid-20th century did not resolve it

but, on the contrary, could make it more aggressive, especially when national factors were combined with religion (conflict: Catholic-Protestant, Islamic, religious-Christian, Jewish).

2) Anti-imperialists in the third world: Terrorism associated with liberation movements (e.g., the Mau Mau in Kenya and Kashmir before independence, Palestinian terrorist groups). With the inability to resolve fundamental conflict issues and the globalization of imperialism, such movements also become global. This includes groups like Osama bin Laden's terrorist organization, Al-Qaeda.

3) Social-revolutionary terrorism: Since the 19th century, terrorist acts were primarily used against the government by extreme revolutionaries and anarchist organizations. In the Russian Empire, individual terrorism was used by secret societies for the will of the people. Among conspiratorial terrorists were Ukrainians like S. Stepniak-Kravchynsky, A. Zhelezniak, S. Perovska, and others. Until the end of 1917, the Bolsheviks used terrorism more selectively and systematically. In the 1920s, well-known groups were the Red Army of Western Germany, the Red Brigades of

Italy, the Japanese Red Army, and several groups in the United States. By the mid-1960s, these «new left» groups posed serious challenges not only to the regime but to the entire social structure of capitalist countries.

4) Right-wing terrorism: Aims to abolish parliamentary democracy and establish an authoritarian system or dictatorship. At the same time, right-wing groups oppose the «new left» (e.g., Italy), consider their actions a threat to society, and choose the right path.

5) Racial and ethnic terrorism: Consists of racial oppression, biological extermination of the inhabitants of the native city, and their replacement by immigrants.

6) Destructive terrorism organized by the intelligence services of a hostile country: Destructive terrorist groups often rely on the «fifth column» of the enemy country and carry out provocative actions.

7) Technological terrorism involving weapons of mass destruction or their components, other harmful substances, electromagnetic agents, computer systems, and communication networks, envisioning the capture, destruction, and disposal of potentially dangerous terrorism, which directly or indirectly poses a threat to an emergency.

Please note that this information is provided for reference and educational purposes and does not promote or support terrorism in any form.

Some believe that criminal terrorism also distinguishes itself from organized crime syndicates, but in most cases, it lacks a clearly defined political objective as it is primarily driven by profit-seeking motives (economic motivation).

The development of terrorism is a result of active social stratification, ideological boundaries, and the formation of political movements. Terrorism as a global phenomenon emerged in the second half of the 19th century. For instance, in the Russian Empire in 1881, the People's Volunteer Army assassinated Emperor Alexander II after several attempts. In 1894, an Italian anarchist killed the President of France, Sadi Carnot. In 1898, anarchists fatally wounded the Austrian Empress Elizabeth and killed the Prime Minister of Spain, Antonio Canovas. In 1900, terrorists killed Italian King Umberto I, and in 1901, President of the United States William McKinley. In Russia, from 1902 to 1907, the Socialist Revolutionaries and other terrorists carried out approximately 5500 terrorist acts, including assassinations of members of the Duma, military police, police, and prosecutors. Terrorism became a key issue in international politics, with most leaders of the most industrialized countries making it their top priority when they met in 1900.

From 1920 to 1939, Ukrainian underground organizations UPA and OUN engaged in individual terrorism against Polish officials (attempted assassinations of Józef Piłsudski, S. Sobinski, Tadeusz Golok, Bronisław Pieracki, and the killing of Deputy Consul O. Maylov, among others). They also targeted Ukrainians (poet Sidor Tverdochlib, the murder of teacher Ivan Baba). Other underground terrorist acts included bombings of Polish government institutions, expropriations, and arson of landholdings. These actions were planned as a response to Poland's anti-Ukrainian policies and to create an atmosphere of internal mobilization within Ukrainian society, but they remained sporadic.

The statistics of terrorist attacks were first published by American historian Alexander Motyl in «Political Violence by Ukrainian Nationalists in Poland During the War» (an anti-communist publication in the

«East European Quarterly»). His data indicates 63 murders between 1921 and 1939. The victims included 36 Ukrainians (including 1 communist), 25 Poles, 1 Russian, and 1 Jew.

On September 25, 1921, during the opening ceremony of the «Eastern Fair» in Lviv, 22-year-old Stepan Fedak-Dym shot Marshal Józef Piłsudski but mistakenly attacked Voivode Kazimierz III. Stepan Fedak was sentenced to six years in prison, while other suspects were released from prison due to a lack of evidence. Fedak was released from prison on August 12, 1924, after numerous appeals by his defense, following the resignation of the Polish Minister of Justice.

On March 22, 1932, militant Yuriy Berezynskyi shot Lviv resident, policeman E. Chekhovsky, who had brutally interrogated political prisoners. Law enforcement authorities could not identify the perpetrator for a long time. In November 1932, an attack was made on the radical OUN post in Horodok, aimed at expropriating gold, but it failed. Yuri Berezynskyi was wounded and killed himself, while Vasyl Bilas and Dmytro Danylshyn were arrested and hanged after a high-profile trial.

In January 1933, Stepan Bandera led the regional leadership of the OUN in Western Ukraine. Prominent OUN historian P. Mirchuk associated this appointment with a change in the form of struggle. Instead of robbing mail and raising money, UPA and OUN fighters instilled fear in their opponents. In October 1933, the head of the Soviet consulate in Lviv, Oleksiy Maylov, was killed. People claim that although Maylov was only the consulate's secretary, he was an OUN activist and, more importantly, an official representative of Joseph Stalin, overseeing the Soviet diplomatic mission led by the Soviet Union. Considering him a consul, the militants shot at him twice, injuring his bodyguards, throwing down their weapons, and waiting for the police to arrive. The purpose of the action was to protest against the trial of the Ukrainian community for the Holodomor in the Soviet Union, which was concealed by the Soviet authorities. The trial lasted only one day and sentenced extremist Mykola Lemyk to death, but it was later commuted to life imprisonment as he was a minor.

In May 1934, a terrorist attack occurred at the editorial office of the «Pratsia» newspaper in Lviv, which supported the communist party. In his confession before a Polish court during the Lviv trial in June 1936, S. Bandera explained that it was an empirical and cautious measure aimed at political forces serving Moscow.

On June 15, 1934, Minister of Internal Affairs General Bronislaw Pieracki, one of the prominent figures in peaceful politics, was assassinated. He was killed by Grigoriy Matseyko. On July 25, 1934, after several warnings, Ivan Baby, a former UGA officer who served as the director of the Ukrainian Academic Gymnasium in Lviv and opposed political terrorism, was killed. He also refused to allow students to join the OUN. In another conciliatory message after the attempted assassination of Ivan Baby, Metropolitan Andrei Sheptytsky, while stating that it did not undermine the power of the Polish state but only incited repression against Ukrainians, condemned the activities of the OUN. Leaders of the Ukrainian Central Committee, including Stepan Balan, Vasyl Madli, Milena Ludnytska, and Volodymyr Starosorsky, criticized the idealistic principles and tactics of Ukrainian nationalists.

During World War II, terrorist acts became more frequent. Terrorism became a means of struggle against various opposing groups, often involving uncontrolled elements, where terrorist acts took on forms of revenge or blind violence. In these difficult circumstances, between 1943 and 1945, a bloody conflict unfolded involving innocent victims from Poland and Ukraine, especially in the civilian populations of Volhynia, Kholmshchyna, and Podlaskie. The actions of Ukrainian insurgents against the Polish government in 1945-1946 and their actions against their representatives among the people were more of a self-defense and liberation uprising than political terrorism.

After the assassination of King Yugoslavia in Marseille in 1934, the French Minister of Foreign Affairs, Louis Jean Barthou, and other foreign ministers, including the Polish Minister of Internal Affairs Bronislaw Pieracki, introduced international sanctions against the Organization of United Nations, specifically sanctions against terrorism. There were also discussions about not providing political asylum to migrants.

The first was the multilateral Geneva Convention on the High Seas, signed on April 29, 1958, which contained numerous articles regarding the fight against terrorism on the high seas or piracy. The Hague Convention of December 16, 1970, on the Suppression of Unlawful Seizure of Aircraft, and the Montreal Convention of September 23, 1971, on Offenses and Certain Other Acts Committed on Board Aircraft, were enacted to control unlawful actions against civil aviation.

On December 14, 1973, a treaty on the prevention and punishment of crimes against persons enjoying international protection, including diplomats, was adopted. The Convention on Combating Terrorism was signed in Strasbourg on January 26, 1977, after extensive discussions in the Council of Europe.

Since 1973, the United Nations has established a Special Committee on Terrorism that operates in three main areas:

- Development and coordination of legal norms, including the drafting of international treaties and contracts.

- Identification and investigation of the root causes of terrorism.

- Development of measures to combat terrorism.

Regarding examples of state terrorism, one could include actions like the installation of a New Year tree in Kyiv during the Euromaidan as a pretext to clear Independence Square of Euromaidan protesters, which resulted in the violent beating of students.

2.2 Nuclear terrorism is the greatest threat to humanity

Military and terrorist acts pose the most significant threat to human rights. Imagine a scenario where human rights are either tightly controlled or considered a «collateral damage» in the event of a mass explosion that causes direct injuries, illnesses, hardships, homelessness, or death. All human rights are compromised in times of war, especially when conflicts persist for several years. The healthcare system collapses, affecting education, housing, employment, the right to food and water, the legal system, freedom of the press and speech, and the accountability of the state or the «enemy» state for violations of these rights, which are severely restricted and even isolated. However, legal protection remains insufficient even in peacetime. During war, the rights of children, women, ethnic minorities, and refugees remain vulnerable.

War and terrorism are truly a descent of humanity. They undermine and restrict the values that underlie human rights and weaken the legal system designed to protect them. However, even during this decline, human rights continue to function to some extent. While they may not overcome all evil, they offer at least minimal protection and some hope for justice.

Due to national wars and emergencies, a state can «suspend» or temporarily postpone some of its guarantees of human rights. However, certain human rights, such as the right to life, freedom from torture, and the right to be free from cruel or degrading treatment, should never be overshadowed. These rights are fundamental and so vital that we must ensure their preservation, even when national security is at stake.

In 2011, the European Court of Human Rights (Al-Skeini and Others v. UK) ruled that the United Kingdom violated Article 2 of the European Convention on Human Rights and Fundamental Freedoms, which defines the right to life. This ruling related to the treatment of civilians during security operations in Basra, Iraq. This was the first case where European Union treaties of wartime were effectively applied on foreign territory and in other regions. In other cases, the treatment of prisoners of war in prison is equated with torture.

War and terrorism have many similarities. Both phenomena are motivated by political, idealistic, or strategic goals and involve extreme violence initiated by one group of people against another. The consequences of war and terrorism are deliberate and catastrophic for individuals. War is more widespread, and its consequences are more destructive and massive. War is waged at the state level, which has all the weapons. Terrorist groups rarely have access to the technical and financial resources of a state.

However, aside from the method and scale of violence, war and terrorism are treated differently under international law. The differences are not always clear-cut, and even experts have different views on whether cases of mass violence are related to terrorism, civil war, unrest, self-defense, legitimate self-determination, or other phenomena.

A nuclear explosion is the process of splitting heavy nuclei. To trigger a reaction, at least 10 kg of highly enriched plutonium is required. This material is not naturally occurring. It is the result of a reaction created in a nuclear reactor. Natural uranium contains about 0.7% of the isotope U-235, with the rest being uranium-238. To conduct a reaction, the material must contain at least 90% uranium-235.

Depending on the objectives to be achieved with nuclear weapons, the nature and location of the objects to be attacked, and the nature of future hostilities, nuclear explosions can occur in the air, above ground (water), and underground. Thus, we distinguish the following types of nuclear explosions:

- Air (high and low).

- Ground-based

- Underground.

The shock waves are often the primary factor of a nuclear explosion's impact. In essence, it is similar to the shockwave of a conventional explosion but lasts longer and is much more destructive. The shockwaves from a nuclear explosion can injure people far from the explosion's center, destroy buildings, and damage military equipment. Shockwaves are areas of intense air compression that spread rapidly in all directions from the explosion's center.

The speed of its propagation depends on the air pressure ahead of the shock wave. It greatly exceeds the speed of sound near the center of the explosion but sharply decreases with increasing distance from the explosion site. In the first 2 seconds, the shockwave travels about 1000 meters, 5 seconds – 2000 meters, and 8 seconds – approximately 3000 meters.

The impact of shockwaves on humans and the destructive effect on military equipment, engineering structures, and material resources are primarily determined by the excessive pressure and the speed of the frontal movement of air. Unprotected individuals are also surprised by the scattering of glass fragments that quickly fly, fallen trees, and the dispersal of military equipment, rocks, and other objects that can be propelled by the rapid pressure of explosive waves.

The greatest indirect damage is observed in populated areas and forests. In these cases, army losses can be greater than from the direct impact of the shockwave. Shockwaves can also cause damage inside buildings by penetrating cracks and openings. Damage from the impact can be classified as light, moderate, severe, and very severe. Light injuries are characterized by temporary damage to hearing organs, frequent minor bruises, and limb dislocations.

Severe injuries are characterized by severe bruising all over the body. This can damage the organs of the head and abdomen, cause profuse nasal and ear bleeding, and also lead to serious fractures and dislocations of limbs. The extent of damage caused by the shockwave depends primarily on the power and type of nuclear explosion. An airburst with a power of 20 kT can cause injuries at distances of up to 2.5 km from the center of the explosion, up to 2 km from the moderate to 2 km, and up to 1.5 km from the strong. With an increase in the caliber of the nuclear bomb, the radius of the shockwave impact increases proportionally to the cube root of the explosion.

In the case of an underground explosion, the shockwave is formed on the ground, and in the case of an underwater explosion, it occurs underwater. In addition, in these types of explosions, some of the energy is used to create shockwaves in the air. Shockwaves that spread on the ground damage underground structures, sewage, and water supply systems. If it spreads underwater, it damages the underwater part of the ship far from the explosion site.

The light emitted from a nuclear explosion is a stream of radiant energy, including ultraviolet, visible, and infrared radiation. The source of light is the bright area consisting of hot explosive products and hot air.

The brightness of the light emission in the first second is multiple times that of the sun. The absorbed energy of the light radiation is converted into heat, leading to the heating of the surface layer of the material.

The radiation is intense enough to ignite or set fire to combustible materials, shatter or melt fuel, and cause massive fires. The impact of the light radiation from a nuclear explosion corresponds to the mass use of incendiary weapons discussed in the fourth educational question. The skin membranes of a person also absorb the energy of light radiation. It can also cause burns due to high temperatures. Burns occur on open parts of the body exposed to the explosion. The gaze of unprotected eyes in the direction of the explosion can damage your eyes and lead to complete loss of vision.

Burns from light exposure are equivalent to burns from fire or scalding. The closer to the explosion, the stronger they are. In the case of an airburst of 20 kT ammunition and an atmospheric transparency of approximately 25 km, burning is observed within a radius of 4.2 km from the center of the explosion. If a charge of 1 MgT explodes, this distance increases to 22.4 km. For 20 kT and 1 MgT ammunition, second-degree burns were observed at distances of 2.9 km and 14.4 km, and third-degree burns at distances of 2.4 km and 12.8 km, respectively.

Missing radiation is an invisible stream of gamma rays and neutrons emitted from the nuclear explosion zone. Gamma rays and neutrons propagate in all directions from the explosion center, reaching hundreds of meters.

As the distance from the explosion increases, the number of gamma rays and neutrons passing through ground units decreases. In the case of underground and underwater nuclear explosions, the effect of transmitted radiation extends over significantly shorter distances compared to surface and air bursts. This is due to the absorption of neutrons and gamma rays by water.

The affected area from missing radiation in medium and high-yield nuclear explosions is somewhat smaller than the affected areas from shockwaves and light radiation. Conversely, for low-yield explosives

(1000 tons or less of TNT equivalent), the area of influence due to prompt radiation surpasses the areas affected by shockwaves and light radiation.

The primary effect of penetrating radiation is determined by the ability of gamma rays and neutrons to ionize atoms in the medium through which they propagate. When passing through living tissue, gamma rays and neutrons ionize atoms and molecules within cells, disrupting important functions of individual organs and systems. Ionization in the body leads to a biological process of cell death and degradation.

As a result, individuals exposed to radiation develop a specific condition known as radiation sickness. The concept of radiation dose (or radiation dose) using X-rays as a unit of measurement was introduced to assess the ionization of surrounding atoms and, consequently, the impact of penetrating radiation on living organisms.

A radiation dose of 1 gray corresponds to the creation of about 2 billion pairs of ions in 1 cubic centimeter of air. Depending on the radiation dose, three degrees of radiation sickness are distinguished. The first (mild) degree occurs when a person receives a dose of

100-200 gray. It is characterized by general weakness, slight nausea, short-term dizziness, and increased perspiration. Typically, individuals do not die from such a radiation dose.

The second (moderate) degree of radiation sickness occurs at doses of 200-300 gray. Symptoms include severe headaches, fever, discomfort in the gastrointestinal tract, and these symptoms gradually worsen, leading to death in most cases.

The third (severe) measurement of radiation sickness occurs at doses above 300 gray. It is characterized by severe headaches, nausea, general weakness, dizziness, and other disturbances. In such cases, very few people survive, and even they remain disabled for life.

Radioactive contamination of humans, military equipment, the environment, and various objects occurs due to the dispersion of charged substances and unreacted parts of the charge that fell from the explosion cloud. The activity of scattered fragments quickly decreases over time, especially in the first hours after the explosion.

For example, in the case of a 20 kT nuclear ammunition explosion, the cumulative activity of scattered fragments is thousands of times less than it was just a minute after the explosion. In the event of a nuclear ammunition explosion, some of the charged substance is not scattered but decomposes into various chemical elements. Its decay involves the formation of alpha particles.

This radioactive decay occurs due to the radioisotopes that form in the soil when exposed to neutrons released during the explosion of atomic nuclei of chemical elements in the soil. Most of the formed isotopes are typically beta-active, and many of their decays are accompanied by gamma rays.

Most long-lived isotopes are retained in radioactive clouds that form after the explosion. The height of the cloud from a 10 kT yield ammunition is 6 km, and the height of a 10 Mg yield ammunition cloud is 25 km. During the movement of the cloud, the largest particles fall out of the cloud and then become smaller and smaller, forming a zone of radioactive contamination along the path of movement, known as the fallout path. The size of the fallout path primarily depends on the power and wind speed of nuclear ammunition and can reach hundreds of meters in length and tens of kilometers in width.

Internal radiation exposure is caused by the entry of radioactive substances into the body through the respiratory and gastrointestinal tracts. Radiation directly interacts with internal organs and can cause severe radiation injuries. The nature of the disease depends on the amount of radioactive material that enters the body. Weapons, military equipment, and engineering structures are not affected by radioactive materials.

Electromagnetic pulses mainly affect electrons and electronic devices. An electromagnetic pulse is a strong electric field created in a very short time.

Hiroshima and Nagasaki. During the spring of 1945, many Japanese endured constant attacks by American B-29 bombers. These planes were virtually invulnerable and flew at altitudes unreachable by Japanese aircraft. For example, one such attack claimed the lives of 125,000 residents of Tokyo, another 100,000, and on March 6, 1945, Tokyo was completely devastated. The American leadership feared that further raids would not be aimed at demonstrating their new weapon.

Therefore, four pre-selected cities – Hiroshima, Kokura, Niigata, and Nagasaki – were not bombed. At 5:23 AM on August 5, the first atomic bomb in history was dropped. The strike was almost perfect. The bomb detonated 200 meters from the target. Many people were busy preparing breakfast, so small charcoal stoves were lit all over the city during this period.

All these stoves were overturned by the explosion, leading to numerous fires far from the epicenter. Residents were supposed to take shelter in temporary shelters, but for several reasons, this did not happen. Firstly, there was no warning, and secondly, a group of planes that did not drop the bomb had already flown over Hiroshima.

After the initial flash, other problems arose. First and foremost was the impact of the blast wave. It traveled at a speed of 800 km/h. Except for a few walls, everything within a 4 km diameter circle was destroyed. The dual effect of the heat and blast waves caused thousands of fires in just a few seconds.

Within minutes of the waves, a strange black rain fell. This phenomenon was related to the fact that the fireball converted the moisture in the atmosphere into steam. It condensed into clouds gathering in the sky. When this cloud, containing water vapor and tiny dust particles, rose and reached colder atmospheric layers, the water condensed again and fell as rain.

People caught in the fireball within 800 meters of the epicenter were severely burned and turned to dust. Those who survived seemed even more terrifying than the dead. They were completely burned by the flash, and the blast wave tore their charred skin.

Out of 76,000 buildings in Hiroshima, 70,000 were completely damaged, 6,820 were destroyed, and 55,000 burned down. Most hospitals were destroyed, leaving only 10% of medical staff. Those who survived began to experience a strange illness, characterized by vomiting and anorexia. Afterward, fever, drowsiness, and fatigue set in. The blood showed a small number of white blood cells. All these were the initial signs of radiation exposure.

The second bombing was scheduled for August 12, after the successful atomic bombing of Hiroshima.

However, since meteorologists predicted worsening weather, it was decided to bomb on August 9. The destination was the city of Kokura. The American plane arrived at the city around 8:30 in the morning, but the bombing of the steel plant was halted. It had been attacked the previous day, and it was still burning. The plane turned toward Nagasaki. At 11:02, the bomb nicknamed «Fat Man» was dropped on the city. It exploded at an altitude of 567 meters.

Two atomic bombs dropped on Japan killed over 200,000 people in a matter of seconds. Many people were exposed to radiation, leading to radiation injuries, cataracts, cancer, and infertility.

That's why nuclear weapons pose a significant threat to all of humanity. According to American experts, the explosion of a 20-Mt thermonuclear bomb could compare to destroying all buildings within a 24 km radius around the Earth and annihilating all life forms within 140 km from the epicenter. Considering the accumulation of nuclear weapons and their destructive power, experts believe that a nuclear world war would result in the deaths of hundreds of millions of people and would obliterate all the achievements of world civilization and culture. Fortunately, the end of the Cold War has somewhat eased the international political situation. Many agreements on the cessation of nuclear tests and the reduction of nuclear weapons have been signed. Another crucial issue today is the safe operation of nuclear power plants. After all, a simple breach of safety measures can have the same consequences as a nuclear war. Today, people need to think about their future and the world they will live in for decades.

Among the modern manifestations of nuclear terrorism, we can mention the actions of the Russian Federation on the territory of Ukraine, where a full-scale war has unfolded. For instance, on March 4, 2020, Russian forces shelled one of the units of the Zaporizhzhia Nuclear Power Plant, resulting in a fire. Fortunately, a catastrophe was averted. It's worth noting that the Zaporizhzhia Nuclear Power Plant is the most powerful nuclear power plant in Europe and the sixth-largest in the world. Furthermore, occupiers damaged the power line supplying electricity to the spent nuclear fuel storage facility at the Chornobyl Nuclear Power Plant at the end of March 2022. In late April 2022, two Kalibr cruise missiles flew towards one of the units of the

Khmelnytskyi Nuclear Power Plant. The Russian Federation has also frequently indirectly threatened Western European countries with a nuclear strike.

CHAPTER 3. INTERNATIONAL TERRORISM AS A FORM OF POLITICAL TERRORISM

3.1 Preconditions for the Emergence of International Terrorism

Despite the significant differences in the historical conditions of the existence of individual nations and peoples at the present stage of social development, the world and its regions consistently witness the widespread use of violence, including terrorism. Various long-term social processes and political struggles are taking place.

First and foremost, we must mention these various processes because the world is characterized by:

- A significant imbalance in the needs and interests of various social groups and nations.

- The spread of radicalism in political ideology and political struggle.

- The resurgence and deepening of economic and political inequality, dictatorship, and colonial tendencies in international relations.

- The emergence of nationalism and religious extremism as global political factors.

- Sharp polarization in the distribution of power in the world.

- The painful process of transitioning from totalitarianism to democracy.

The current situation and the use of terrorism in political struggles at both the «internal» and international levels significantly alter its content, organization, and tactics. Under the influence of these conditions, over the past decade of the 20th century, more or less clear trends have emerged in the development of terrorism. Research in this field is essential for understanding its role as a global threat to humanity, many countries, and science itself. Developing measures necessary for effective counteraction is crucial.

The first major trend in contemporary terrorism, characteristic of many countries worldwide, is the steady growth of international relations, international security, and social threats to constitutional order and citizens' rights. According to intelligence agencies, international terrorism in 1998-1993 was characterized by such indicators (the first number represents the number of attacks, and the second represents the number of victims): Africa – 175 and 758, Asia – 410 and 1172, Eurasia (the former Soviet territory) – 22 and 10, Latin America – 915 and 769, the Middle East – 513 and 783, North America – 10 and 1008, Western Europe – 818 and 806. 2000 saw an increase in the number of terrorist attacks worldwide from 392 to 423 compared to 1999. The number of casualties also increased: 405 killed and 791 injured (233 and 706, respectively, in 1999).

The world situation over the last 15-20 years indicates that terrorism has reached an astonishing speed. The change in terrorist strategies and tactics, methods of influence, motivational systems, has revealed several new types of this phenomenon. Contemporary practice shows that terrorism is becoming increasingly widespread, amorphous, and harder to counter.

Right and left-wing extremism, along with known societies, including class-related contradictions, that have triggered international terrorism in Western countries, the market models of the social order, and certain contemporary situations. This is becoming increasingly dangerous. New contradictions are also long-term. Some of them have a socio-economic and political basis, have a significant impact on many countries' social systems, and are associated with significant migration processes linked to serious ethnic conflicts.

Researchers of the reasons for the rapid spread of terrorism worldwide, despite active counterterrorism efforts in various parts of the world, have primarily focused on the external aspects of the matter. For most people today, terrorists are individuals in black masks with guns who shout incomprehensible words. The rest of the public debate is about how to defend against these individuals.

Terrorism, as a form of violence, primarily aims to achieve specific goals and pursue personal ambitions in self-interest. From a methodological standpoint, it doesn't matter what attire it wears, whether it's based on nationality, religion, or other factors. However, its essence remains unchanged – it is armed struggle. Therefore, it can be confidently stated that the essence of terrorism lies in the use of extreme violence to achieve specific political objectives. People who use terrorism as a form of political violence can come from various social backgrounds, meaning specific social groups or populations.

The foundation for the recruitment of individuals into terrorism lies in the social status of societal relations and the large strata of the population, such as classes. The social status of the masses today is characterized by a continuous process of poverty, alienation, and massification. This process is common in most Asian and African countries, including the former Soviet countries, especially in regions like the North Caucasus with the highest levels of unemployment and complete economic infrastructure collapse.

Those who are unemployed and lack means of survival are willing to do anything to support their families, including engaging in criminal activities, at least if it provides for their basic needs. These segments of the population form the primary social base for all forms of crime, including terrorism. However, poverty alone is not the main cause of terrorism. Poor people do not have access to weapons and explosives to defend their rights. Someone needs to invest significant resources to make such possibilities available to the masses. Of course, they do not pay for themselves; they use the slogan of idealism to direct terrorist actions towards their goals. Terrorist leaders recognize the need to overcome the explosive potential of marginalized social groups. To do this, they must identify and target their enemies and mobilize the anger of all against them.

Nationalism and religious extremism are entirely consistent with this goal for several reasons:

- They allow the true goals of a political party or its leader, who determines the interests of a group, clan, or personal interests, to be disguised.

- They give protests a systematic political character.

- They identify an enemy and unite all their protest potential in the fight against them.

What is happening in Islamic countries, especially in the North Caucasus, such as Chechnya?

Neither Islam nor the national self-awareness of people causes radicalism. It is about their exploitation for political purposes. In the Caucasus, Wahhabism has become one such form of masking, as one of the «pure» Islamic directions.

Equally dangerous is nationalist activity, often carried out under the banner of the National Liberation Movement. Here, as in the previous case, there is no direct internal connection but an external convergence, allowing political violence and its extreme forms to be successfully concealed within a state liberation struggle.

Judging from the behavior of terrorists, including suicide bombers, through the prism of these traits, their fanatical behavior is grounded not in the terrorists' goals (terrorism is just a means) but in the righteousness of their cause before Allah, on behalf of his people. Terrorism requires sacrifice. Without it, it cannot address a serious problem. People intoxicated by religious and nationalist ideologies, especially the youth, sincerely believe in their mission and identify their lives and destinies not with fear but with the ideals of nationalism and religious idealism. Unfortunately, media propaganda has not found words or arguments to expose this self-deception. Today, propagandistic work requires a different approach. It not only reveals the inhuman nature of terrorism but also clarifies the essence of the matter through images, statements, and discussions accessible to the general public.

Contemporary terrorism is widely spread, has an organized structure, its own financial system, and headquarters that coordinate various seemingly diverse activities related to the mission and purpose of the terrorist organization. Recognizing the international nature of contemporary terrorism, it becomes evident that effective international coordination is also necessary in combating it.

The phenomenon of terrorism is often idealized as having cultural or religious origins. We even talk about a «clash of civilizations.» Some say that certain cultures are prone to terrorism. In reality, nobody is a «terrorist» by nature. Terrorism is not the goal but a means to an end. These methods can be used by anyone, from individuals to states. Furthermore, «terrorist idealism» – the ideological system that propagates and justifies terrorism (e.g., so-called «Islamic fundamentalism») – is part of the terrorist arsenal, just like Kalashnikov rifles. Therefore, considering Islam as a «terrorist doctrine» doesn't make sense. Propaganda that glorifies terrorism can manipulate anything if necessary, including peaceful aspects such as the environment. The world is more familiar with Islamic terrorism than others simply because ISIS employs terrorist methods for various reasons.

On the other hand, it is also true that terrorism is a mindset. Terrorists usually cooperate and work well together, regardless of the ideals they are fighting for.

The main reason for the existence of terrorism lies in its effectiveness. As long as a few individuals with guns and explosives can impose their will on the state, there will always be people willing to exploit this. Some people know how to take advantage of the situation that arises in a country during terrorist attacks.

Terrorist attacks against democracy: In non-democratic countries, government officials are often the victims of terrorist acts. In religious societies, terrorists may threaten sacred sites, while in secular societies, they may target objects of national pride. However, in today's world, the most common targets of terrorist attacks are the general public. This is due to three situations. Firstly, in any country, ordinary people have the least protection against armed violence, while government officials, holy sites, and valuable property are usually well-guarded. Secondly, most terrorist attacks have a democratic character where the lives of the general public are considered paramount. In such countries, societies usually believe that governments that cannot protect their citizens are failing in their duties and need to be replaced. Thirdly, democratic regimes typically practice humanitarian methods of punishment. Even if a terrorist attack fails, the perpetrator has a chance of surviving. Furthermore, the families of terrorists, their friends, ideological inspirations, and sympathizers are safe – and for fanatical terrorists, this can be even more important than their own well-being.

Thus, the combination of social unrest, cultural conflicts, and psychological anger increases the number of threats in the world and compares them to unexpected natural disasters, turning society into a quasi-natural community.

In addition, in recent years, various irrational organizations that openly advocate violence have emerged. The most typical examples of such organizations are the Japanese cult Aum Shinrikyo, which claimed responsibility for the Tokyo subway attack in March 1995, and the American state that bombed a building in Oklahoma in April 1995.

One of the reasons for the spread of international terrorism is the sharp change in its nature. Terrorism evolves and thrives as a tool for broader conflicts. As a traditional tool of idealistic struggle (right-wing/left-wing terrorism), it acquires a «civilized character,» and in «civilized internal conflicts,» it becomes an attractive tool for small groups seeking disproportionate influence.

The cause of the international terrorism epidemic is the changing terrorist environment, making contemporary society increasingly vulnerable. Information about killings, murders, accidents, and so on, is constantly spreading, which sometimes makes people less sensitive to almost daily terrorist acts. As a result, terrorist organizations that seek public attention and compete are increasingly resorting to more dramatic and violent behavior, a trend that is likely to intensify in the future. This is because technological advancements and information technology make it easier for terrorists to acquire knowledge of modern weapons and bomb-making at home. Furthermore, advanced societies in various fields (defense, trade, banking, transportation, etc.) are increasingly reliant on electronic governance and communications. This has led to the emergence of so-called «social islands.» In other words, a group of people who feel alienated because they lack access to information, people who have moved out of the information age.

Terrorism is increasingly merging with the complex sector of organized crime.

After the Cold War, the legitimacy of many European, Asian, and African nations has been increasingly questioned by both ethnic and religious groups, as well as by movement-based national and supranational «self-determination» organizations. The level of instability and violence is growing due to the increasing number of non-state entities challenging the principles of national sovereignty.

The reasons for the escalation of international terrorism include the ineffectiveness of international legal instruments to combat terrorism and the state as the primary subject of international law in this field of international law.

As a second major trend of terrorism, it is necessary to emphasize the importance of long-term factors in contemporary political life, which are a relatively stable phenomenon in the development of society. Over the past decades, terrorism has transformed into not only a widespread phenomenon in socio-political relations in significant parts of the world but also active efforts towards regionalization and eradication in both individual countries and global societies, while acquiring social stability.

Contemporary terrorist practices have undergone a qualitative change in their significance as a means of socio-political violence in international and domestic relations. Although in recent years, terrorism has been generally characterized as a tactical tool, contemporary socio-political realities show that its significance has fundamentally escalated to a strategic level.

Terrorism inflicts mass casualties, exerts strong psychological pressure on a large number of people, sometimes leads to the destruction of irreparable material and spiritual values, fosters enmity between nations, triggers wars, influences social and national relations, generates distrust, and hatred among target groups, which may be insurmountable for an entire generation. Terrorism is a form of war and a highly effective one. Not all enemy attacks can be blocked without additional losses. Terrorism is a constant companion of humanity, one of the most dangerous and unpredictable phenomena of our time, which is taking on increasingly diverse forms and threatening dimensions.

In the 20th century, the motives for using terrorism have significantly expanded. If Russian populists and Social Revolutionaries saw terrorism as self-sacrifice for the benefit of society, Italian «Red Brigades» used it as a method and a means of self-assertion. Fascist neo-Nazi «red terrorism» and «black» terrorism have nothing to do with the fall of the People's Volunteer Army. Contemporary terrorism has one common goal, which is the seizure of power. There is no talk of any «social good» in this context.

With the development of unprecedented high technologies and the creation of global technological systems and networks (railways, airlines, electric power generation, nuclear technologies, computer networks, etc.), terrorism has become highly efficient and «widespread.» The Western world is now entirely dependent on them. A century and a half ago, there were no such technologies on Earth, so there were no serious threats.

The dispersion of a dangerous infection in one container of water can cause an epidemic in many countries around the world, not just in one city. Sending laboratory strains of Siberian plague, which are not adapted for bacterial warfare, seems like child's play compared to a combat sample of biological weapons or a computer virus that disrupts the automated control system of a nuclear power plant.

However, it is not only the scale of contemporary terrorism and its technological globalization. Today, terrorist acts are carried out through mass media, especially through electronic means, becoming global. After all, the nightmares of New York skyscrapers were witnessed by the whole world through television and the internet, causing fear globally. Humanity is clearly entering a new phase of life restructuring, and terrorism plays a leading role in this transformation as a universal threat to nations and communities. Of course, television and the internet are not for such a terrifying act, but their goal is simply to create a favorable environment for the spread of information about terrorism. This issue is increasingly attracting the attention of experts and authorities.

«In the end, the public reaction is the most important, and often the only goal of terrorists,» said the chief editor of the popular Ukrainian weekly «Spiegel der Woche» in his speech. In this situation, journalists are not just independent witnesses but actively participate in what is happening, whether they want to or not. They disseminate information. The main criteria for selecting journalists should be professionalism and responsibility, the ability to anticipate the consequences of their actions rather than working according to the publication's schedule.

On June 20, 2005, the Council of Europe adopted a resolution on the media and terrorism, encouraging journalists to create a unified set of rules for reporting on terrorist attacks. In the main part of the resolution, the Congress calls on journalists not to promote terrorist targets, not to incite panic often caused by terrorist acts, and not to allow terrorists to communicate with a wide audience.

The world is already threatened by nuclear terrorism and terrorism involving the use of toxic substances. Kidnapping people for the purpose of extortion or ransom has become an epidemic. Many people today feel all the «incentives» of information terrorism. At the beginning of the 21st century, one can speak about the history and geography of terrorism only in a fairly common understanding – terrorism knows no borders between countries and nature anymore. The globalization of terrorism has often led to several terrorist groups in different countries participating in the preparation and execution of terrorist attacks. For example, the Arab Al-Qaeda, the Basque Homeland and Liberty, the Irish IRA, the Corsican Mafia, but there are special centers worldwide that can focus on terrorist activities at any time and prepare for it. Typically, such centers are located in countries or regions where serious conflicts are taking place (Palestine, Ulster, the Basque Country), or in countries or regions where the authorities do not have sufficient control over their territory and, therefore, cannot conduct comprehensive anti-terrorist training (Afghanistan, Colombia, Indonesia). There are many main sources of funding for global terrorism.

Terrorism is a crime against public safety, directed at the individual, society, and the nation. Terrorism does not arise in a vacuum, but there are certain conditions and conditions of social life that contribute to this. It tends to grow during transitional phases of society when society objectively creates conditions for social conflicts characterized by inadequate assessment of reality, a widespread sense of insecurity, and unmet expectations, shaping a special state of collective consciousness. Social anxiety, resentment, and attacks. In such situations, calls for social protest are easily perceived by radicals. When this is exacerbated by the weakness of state power, the inability to ensure the physical security of individuals and their property, the cult of violence begins to develop rapidly, and radicalism in these situations is an integral part of the spirit of society. Let's now define the main contradictions and factors that influence the nature and trends of terrorism today.

First of all, it is the contradiction of an economic nature, the main contradictions of which are currently: a serious mismatch between the consequences of economic reforms and social expectations, disproportionately high costs of reforms (poverty of the majority of the population).

All of this is influenced by long-term factors such as uncontrolled price increases, unemployment, the shrinking of domestic markets, and the displacement of domestic producers, entrepreneurial difficulties, and economic criminalization. Against the backdrop of limited financial, material-technical, resource, and other capabilities, they have serious social consequences, laying the foundation for social tension and, consequently, political extremism.

Social contradictions have acquired special significance in modern social reality.

Firstly, it is a contradiction arising from the division of society into groups with different economic statuses. On this basis, social polarization has occurred and continues to develop. Income inequality between the richest and poorest countries exceeds the norm, which, of course, does not increase social stability in the world.

Secondly, it is contradictions caused by the deepening of national, religious, regional, and other conflicts that lead to the action of such factors as:

- The formation of a long-term hotbed of social tension and conflicts. This can easily escalate into a stage of open conflict with active use of forms of violence, including terrorism.

- The widespread spread of criminal influence in the state, especially on state bodies. This reduces the effectiveness of law enforcement agencies and increases threats to people and property security.

Thirdly, it is contradictions caused by the destruction of an effective social security system in many countries. Within the framework of these contradictions, such factors as:

- The growth of social dissatisfaction, the rise of egoism, the indifference of society, and so on.

- Certain strata of the population are gradually drawn into criminal activities, most often these are the poorest people in society.

The economic crisis, which largely affects the interests of the middle class, also generates political instability in the form of strikes, pickets, and riots, potentially affecting political relations and professionally organized populations, leading to mass unemployment. Involvement in group activities is the main form of activity due to unemployment due to low qualifications, combined with other factors. Depending on the individual's characteristics (lack of diligence, a desire to get rich quickly, attract attention for a while, become popular among others), individuals and other members of the group actively participate in terrorist activities.

According to the majority of local scholars, it is the economic factor that determines all the features of terrorism.

Thus, there are many forms of global terrorism, but in any form, they are the most dangerous in terms of their scale, unpredictability, and the impact of socio-political problems of the 21st century. If terrorism was a regional phenomenon not so long ago, in the last 10-15 years, it has become global in character, increasingly threatening the security of many countries, exerting strong psychological and political pressure on citizens, causing economic and moral losses.

Terrorism is the most serious problem of our time, which concerns all of humanity, not just one nation, and we must combat it as soon as possible.

As for the prerequisites for the emergence of international terrorism, the first terrorist group in the history of humanity can be considered the sect of the Sicarii, which operated in Palestine from 66 to 73 AD. Its name comes from the name of the favorite weapon of the group – a short sword (sica). It could easily be hidden under clothing. The Sicarii carried out their actions mainly during mass gatherings. They believed that it was most convenient to inflict fatal blows in an uncontrolled crowd. After all, no one could determine with certainty who did it. The «darkness of the crowd» was their element. The main targets of the Sicarii's attacks were representatives of the Egyptian and Palestinian diasporas, who were trying to establish friendly relations with the Roman Empire. The Sicarii were fervent religious fanatics. They bravely endured torture because they believed that after the overthrow of the regime they hated, an era of higher justice would come.

3.2 Global Strategy to Combat International Terrorism

On September 12, 2001, the heads of the European Atlantic Partnership Council (EAPC) strongly condemned the terrorist attacks of September 11, 2001, on the United States and pledged to make every effort to combat terrorism.

Based on this, members of the Euro-Atlantic Partnership Council (EAPC) endorse an anti-terrorism action plan to fulfill their international commitments in this area. They recognize that combating terrorism requires significant coordinated efforts by the international community and, drawing on the successful experience of EAPC cooperation, are determined to make an effective contribution to these efforts.

Within their competencies, EAPC member states, in accordance with universally recognized norms and principles of international law, the Charter of the United Nations, and the provisions of UN Security Council Resolution 1373, prevent and counter terrorism in all its possible forms.

In this regard, EAPC member countries «find ways to enhance and expedite the exchange of operational information, including actions and movements of individual terrorists and their groups,» as well as «coordinate joint efforts between countries and sub-regions.» They support international actions aimed at addressing this serious problem and threat to international security.

In the fight against terrorism, EAPC member states undertake to protect and promote the fundamental rights and freedoms of individuals and the rule of law.

EAPC members reaffirm their readiness to sign, ratify, and implement the United Nations Convention on Terrorism.

In the fight against terrorism within the framework of the EAPC, cooperation should be carried out in accordance with the national security and defense policies of each EAPC member country and the general principles of the EAPC and PfP. Member countries seek to complement the activities of relevant international organizations in this field.

In the context of globalization of international affairs, the fight against terrorism is ineffective at the national level alone. This challenge requires joint efforts of states at parliamentary, governmental, and societal levels. Experts have recognized as prospective and responsible one of the most important NATO policies in the fight against modern terrorism, the main direction of which was defined at the Paris Summit in November 2002 and the Istanbul Summit under the title «Design for Stability.»

Today, we must systematically and internationally combat international terrorism, rather than approach it amateurishly as a threat. It has become clear that combating phenomena like terrorism requires not only one country but a group of countries. Efforts need to be coordinated at the international organization level. In this sense, NATO is the most effective mechanism for combating international terrorism.

Now is the time to create a rapid response system where tens of thousands of well-trained and modernly equipped soldiers work to stay one step ahead of terrorism. Today, this structure is designed to protect the population from acts of terror and countermeasures that could result in the deaths of tens of thousands of people.

International terrorism is a form of brutal confrontation between civilizations in a globalized world. First and foremost, it is about the most radical and aggressive conflict between the Jewish and Islamic civilizations. Christian civilizations, especially their Catholic and Protestant branches, are also drawn into this struggle. However, the Orthodox people have not remained aloof, especially given the expansion of the zone of military conflict to the territory of Iraq.

Military delegations from Orthodox countries, including Bulgaria and Ukraine, are participating in the war in Iraq. We must not forget the features of civilization characteristic of certain parts of Africa, Asia, and Latin America, such as Buddhism and the natural cults of ancient languages.

The sense of civilization development determines its attitude toward human life. The most practical approach to this problem is found in Islamic civilization. Sacrifices of carriers of Islamic values and representatives of other civilizations are considered normal and eternal phenomena. Radical Islamic groups are especially aggressively pursuing these paths. Therefore, international terrorism has become a means for Islamic civilization to enter into a struggle for leading positions in world society and the world economy.

Regarding the issue of human rights protection in the fight against terrorism, there have been many human rights problems arising in the fight against terrorism in recent times. For example, the United Kingdom is ready to amend human rights legislation to combat terrorism. This was recently announced by British Prime Minister Tony Blair at a monthly press conference on Downing Street. He told reporters about the government's plans to simplify and expedite the deportation of foreigners suspected of involvement in terrorism. «The government is prepared to make changes to human rights legislation if there are difficulties in implementing new measures for the deportation of people suspected of or involved in terrorist activities,» the Prime Minister said.

The United Kingdom, which is a party to the European Convention on Human Rights, cannot deport citizens from countries where they face the death penalty or torture. Therefore, according to Blair, the British government is currently engaged in intensive consultations with many countries to ensure humane treatment of the citizens being deported. Blair stated, «We have already signed a memorandum of understanding with Jordan on this issue. Yesterday, I had constructive discussions with the leaders of Algeria and Lebanon. Overall, we are in negotiations with approximately 10 countries.»

The British human rights organization Liberty has already expressed concern about the government's intention to sacrifice human rights in the fight against terrorism. Earlier, the wife of the Prime Minister of the United Kingdom, Cherie Blair, expressed concern that the persecution of terrorists could undermine fundamental human rights.

However, the head of the British cabinet insists on the need for radical measures. «Coming to the United Kingdom is not a walk in the park. People are responsible for life in this country. You must share the values and attitudes toward our way of life. If you act against the country and its people, you don't belong here,» Blair said. «They come here and play by our rules, or they will have to leave,» he added.

How can we fight terrorism today without violating human rights? The issue of combating torture is closely related to terrorism. Currently, this topic is being discussed worldwide. The question of torture and its use, as well as the fight against torture, has been the subject of a very wide-ranging discussion. Currently, the country that effectively sets standards for the world and even for the United Nations is Iraq, particularly the United States, which continues to use and torture prisoners at the Abu Ghraib prison near Baghdad. Is this possible in the war on terrorism? Or is it actually a provocation of terrorist acts by the relatives and friends of the detainees who are violating human rights?

As for Ukraine's participation in the fight against international terrorism, it is socially accompanied by the use of intentional and deliberate violence through hostage-taking, arson, killings, torture, threats to residents and authorities, other abuses, or threats to the lives and health of innocent people.

The legal basis for combating terrorism in Ukraine is the Constitution of Ukraine (254k/96-VR), the Criminal Code of Ukraine (2341-14), this law, other laws of Ukraine, and the European Convention on the Fight against Terrorism. The International Convention for the Suppression of Terrorist Bombings, 1997, the

International Convention for the Suppression of the Financing of Terrorism, 1999, and other international conventions in Ukraine approved by the Verkhovna Rada of Ukraine, as well as decrees and orders of the President of Ukraine, resolutions and orders of the Cabinet of Ministers of Ukraine. The above-mentioned and other legal acts regulate the activities of terrorist organizations on the territory of Ukraine.

The fight against terrorism is based on the following principles:

1. Strict adherence to human rights and the freedoms of citizens.

2. Comprehensive use of legal, political, socio-economic, advocacy, and other means.

3. Inevitable punishment for involvement in terrorist activities.

4. Priority in protecting the lives and rights of individuals vulnerable to terrorism.

5. Combining open and covert methods to combat terrorism.

6. Confidentiality of information about techniques and tactics in the fight against terrorism and the composition of participants.

7. Coordination of command with units and resources involved in counter-terrorism operations.

8. Cooperation with foreign states, their law enforcement agencies, intelligence services, and international organizations engaged in counter-terrorism activities in the war on terrorism.

The entities directly engaged in the fight against terrorism within their capabilities include:

- The Security Service of Ukraine, the main body of the national system for countering terrorist activities.

- The Ministry of Internal Affairs of Ukraine.

- The Ministry of Defense of Ukraine.

- The Ministry of Emergency Situations and Protection of the Population from the Consequences of the Chornobyl Catastrophe.

- The State Border Guard Service of Ukraine.

- The Ministry of Foreign Affairs of Ukraine for the implementation of criminal justice.

- The Ministry of Foreign Affairs of Ukraine.

Ukrainian special services combat terrorism by:

- Conducting operational and investigative measures to prevent, detect, and suppress terrorist activities, including international terrorism.

- Collecting information about the activities of foreign and international terrorist organizations.

- Operating within systems and communication channels that terrorists may use within the limits of the powers defined by current legislation, exclusively for the purpose of obtaining preventive intelligence information in the event of a terrorist attack or a threat to counter terrorism.

- Organizing and conducting counter-terrorism measures and coordinating the activities of individuals involved in counter-terrorism in accordance with the possibilities defined by Ukrainian legislation.

- Conducting pre-trial investigations into offenses related to terrorist activities.

- Ensuring security against terrorist attacks on Ukrainian institutions located outside the territory, their employees, and their families.

The Ministry of Internal Affairs of Ukraine fights terrorism by preventing, detecting, and terminating crimes committed with the aim of terrorism. According to Ukrainian law, the investigation of such crimes falls under the jurisdiction of the Ministry of Internal Affairs. The Antiterrorist Center of the Security Service of

Ukraine is responsible for organizing and conducting anti-terrorism measures and coordinating the activities of individuals focused on counter-terrorism in accordance with the possibilities defined by Ukrainian legislation. The decision to conduct an anti-terrorism operation is made with the written permission of the Secretary of the Security Service of Ukraine, depending on the degree of public danger from a terrorist act. The decision to conduct an anti-terrorism operation must be promptly reported to the President of Ukraine. The public is informed about terrorist acts through the head of the operational center or the person he has entrusted with public relations.

In accordance with signed international agreements, Ukraine cooperates with foreign states, its law enforcement agencies, intelligence services, and international organizations engaged in the fight against international terrorism in the field of counter-terrorism.

Terrorism, unfortunately, has become an integral part of political and economic processes in the world and poses an increasing threat to public and national security, with isolated manifestations evolving into a mass phenomenon. In modern conditions, there is an escalation of terrorist activities not only by extremist organizations and individuals but also by entire states. Moreover, the nature of their actions is becoming more complex, non-standard, and ruthless.

The causes of terrorism can be attributed to the growth of economic crises, the inability of society to regulate complex socio-political processes, rapid changes in human and political ideals, values, and the involvement of a large population with low spirituality, culture, and education in active political life, often devoid of political experience. All of these factors activate the desire to exploit the weaknesses of the social and state systems and find the «shortest» path to achieving their goals.

Recent research and publications have made a significant contribution to the theoretical and methodological foundations and the study of individual aspects of counterterrorism by scholars both in Ukraine and abroad, including V. Krutov, V. Antypenko, A. Doroshenko, V. Lipkan, L. Moshkova, I. Shkurat, Ya. Dashkevych, V. N. Kudryavtsev, V. Tymoshenko, S. Dryomov, Benjamin Jenkins, Ernst Arechaga, Raymond Aron, Eugene Dinstein, and others. At the same time, an analysis of the dynamics of terrorist acts both in Ukraine and worldwide indicates that terrorists are using new forms, means, and demands, highlighting the importance of further research by scholars and practitioners to prevent these disgraceful phenomena.

An antiterrorist operation (ATO) is a complex set of coordinated special measures aimed at preventing, preventing, and terminating terrorist activities, rescuing hostages, ensuring the safety of the population, neutralizing terrorists, and minimizing the consequences of terrorist activities.

The decision to conduct an antiterrorist operation is made depending on the degree of public danger posed by a terrorist act by the head of the Antiterrorist Center at the Security Service of Ukraine with the written permission of the Head of the Security Service of Ukraine or the head of the coordinating group of the relevant regional body of the Security Service of Ukraine with the written permission of the head of the Antiterrorist Center at the Security Service of Ukraine, approved by the Head of the Security Service of Ukraine. The President of Ukraine is promptly informed of the decision to conduct an antiterrorist operation.

Other central and local executive authorities, local self-government bodies, enterprises, institutions, organizations, regardless of their subordination and ownership form, their officials, and citizens, may be involved in antiterrorist operations by the decision of the leadership of the antiterrorist operation and with their consent.

The coordination of the activities of the entities involved in the fight against terrorism is carried out by the Antiterrorist Center at the Security Service of Ukraine.

An antiterrorist operation is considered completed when the terrorist act has been prevented, the threat to the lives and health of hostages and other individuals in the area of its implementation has been eliminated.

The decision to terminate an antiterrorist operation is made by the head of the operational headquarters managing the operation. The ongoing events in Eastern Ukraine, where an antiterrorist operation is still ongoing, provide reason to reconsider not only the terms of conducting the ATO but also to more precisely define the very concept of an antiterrorist operation and its essence.

State bodies, local self-government bodies, citizen associations, organizations, and their officials are obliged to assist the authorities involved in the fight against terrorism, report information they become aware of regarding terrorist activities or any other circumstances, the information about which may contribute to preventing, detecting, and terminating terrorist activities, as well as minimizing its consequences.

The practice of conducting the Anti-Terrorist Operation (ATO) in the East of our country has exposed certain problematic issues, the main of which are expressed in the partial loss of control and coordination of the activities of the above-mentioned subjects of the fight against terrorism, and sometimes the inability to timely and fully perform tasks assigned to them within their competence. This also includes the disregard for the traditions and peculiarities of the development of individual regions of the country, as well as the norms of national and international legislation.

The purpose of this article is to study the impact of the phenomenon of terrorism on the state of national security of the country in the context of modern social and political life and to improve the algorithm of organizing the fight against terrorism. Terrorism is a socially dangerous activity that involves the deliberate, purposeful use of violence through the seizure of hostages, arson, killings, torture, intimidation of the population and authorities, or other acts of aggression against the lives or health of innocent people, or threats to commit criminal actions with the aim of achieving criminal goals.

The mandatory elements that characterize terrorism include the presence of violence, usually armed or the threat of it; causing or threatening to cause harm to human health or material and moral damage; deprivation or the threat of deprivation of human lives. Such actions are capable of causing a wide resonance, leaving a deep mark in the psychology of the population or a significant part of it, undermining the atmosphere of security, peace, and stability in society.

All terrorist acts are accompanied by the use of violence or the threat of violence. Often, this is accompanied by specific demands from terrorists, and the violence they employ is mainly directed against civilian targets. The motives are mostly of a political nature. Actions are carried out in such a way as to attract maximum public attention. Perpetrators are usually members of organized groups, unlike other criminals, they take responsibility for their actions. And, finally, the very action is intended to have an impact beyond causing immediate physical harm.

The legal basis for combating terrorism consists of the Constitution of Ukraine, the Criminal Code of Ukraine, the Law of Ukraine «On Combating Terrorism,» other laws of Ukraine, the European Convention on the Suppression of Terrorism of 1977, the International Convention for the Suppression of Terrorist Bombings of 1997, the International Convention for the Suppression of the Financing of Terrorism of 1999, and other international treaties of Ukraine, for which the consent to be bound has been given by the Verkhovna Rada of Ukraine, as well as decrees of the President of Ukraine, resolutions, and orders of the Cabinet of Ministers of Ukraine, as well as other legislative acts adopted to implement the laws of Ukraine.

Terrorism is a very complex, dynamic, and multifaceted phenomenon. Overcoming it in the 21st century is very difficult, as it has taken on new forms.

However, this does not mean that the fight against criminality is futile. It is imperative to prevent terrorist attacks from becoming a common occurrence, and terrorist demands from becoming the main determinant of foreign policy; this should be the top priority today.

CONCLUSIONS

Through an in-depth examination of this issue, we have made several generalizations and drawn certain conclusions. Terrorism, as a significant and politically meaningful phenomenon, justifies the resort to terror to challenge the legitimacy and rights of the state and achieve their own goals by certain social groups.

The most crucial factor is that the further they go, the more they try to replace human history, an uncontrolled game in which special terrorism is a highly effective tool. They do not believe that this «tool» will somehow get out of control, and the «player» will be able to start playing on their own. Unfortunately, covert operations have become a necessary and widely used instrument in intergovernmental struggles. Never forget that terrorism is a means to get out of control and involve the entire world in the hands of international terrorists.

The main demands of terrorists on a societal scale are the restoration of the state's role and its monopoly on the use of force within society, which pertains to practical tactics and technologies in the fight against terrorism.

At this stage of societal development, the following methods of combating terrorism exist:

- Prevention; blocking terrorism at an early stage and preventing its formation and development;

- Avoiding ideological justification of terror under the banners of «defending the nation's rights,» «defending faith,» and so on;

- Entrusting all anti-terrorist activities to the most reliable intelligence agencies with no interference in their work by any other governing bodies;

- Preparing agreements with terrorists solely by these intelligence agencies and only to cover the preparation of actions for the complete destruction of terrorists;

- No concessions to terrorists, no unpunished acts of terrorism, even if it costs the lives of hostages and innocent people, because practice shows that any success of terrorists provokes further growth of terrorism and the number of victims;

- Special psychological operations by the media portraying the suppression of terrorism as a tragic necessity, contrasting the «blackness» of terrorism with the «purity» of those who fight against it.

The seriousness of modern terrorism has long been recognized by Western democracies, and accordingly, a comprehensive system for combating terrorism has been developed. They have achieved impressive success in many respects. At this stage, the zones of terrorist activity have been completely deactivated and countered by the latest meticulously developed counterterrorism methods.

Back in 1975, the U.S. national security system had so-called special reconnaissance units. For example, the Nuclear Emergency Search Team (NEST) deals directly with nuclear terrorism issues. Although there hasn't been a significant precedent, the U.S. government stated that avoiding a nuclear attack is unlikely.

In this regard, the question arises: will nuclear or bacteriological terrorism become a powerful and perfect deterrent for developing countries in the near future? You can buy or make twelve medium-level nuclear bombs and smuggle them into the United States, and then carry out violence against people and the state on-site. We live in a dynamic and unpredictable world.

Minor obvious mistakes can lead to the demise of all humanity. Therefore, we must recognize that not all problems of our technocratic civilization can be purely technically solved.

It is a mistake to think that terrorism emerged at the end of the 19th century. Terrorism is as old as violence itself. Sporadically and episodically, it has permeated the entire history of humanity. In all nations and at all times, the dialectics of interests created situations where the use of property, freedom, health, and the lives of some people became a means of achieving goals for others. The space between the desired and the real has always been occupied by someone's well-being or someone's life. Evidence of this can be found in the fates of entire nations, rulers, and unknown individuals throughout history.

In Europe, terrorism became a prominent socio-political phenomenon in the 1970s and 1980s. It was during this period that terrorism developed its methodology, technology, and ideology. Russian populism, which transitioned from ineffective socialism propaganda to effective terrorist acts, opened the era of permanent European terrorism. «Narodnaya Volya»

(People's Will) kept the entire system of state power in the Russian Empire in an incredible state of tension for over five years and undoubtedly stimulated the emergence and intensive formation of European terrorism. (Albert Camus, in his book «The Rebel,» writes that in 1892 alone, there were over a thousand dynamite attacks in Europe and about five hundred in America).

The populists were not the first terrorists, but they were the first to create a terrorist organization. Terrorist methods were used before «Narodnaya Volya,» but it was only in this organization that an impersonal mechanism was first objectified, creating the strategy and tactics of terrorist activities, and the continuous process of organizing terrorist acts.

The organizational principles of «Narodnaya Volya» would later become not only a template for terrorist organizations but also for parties like the Russian Social Democratic Labor Party (Bolsheviks) and the National Socialist German Workers' Party (Nazi Party). In formulating the concept of a terrorist organization, the «Executive Committee» of «Narodnaya Volya» started with a clear division of members into supporters of revolutionary transformations (those who theoretically supported the idea of these transformations) and those who practically implemented them. According to the Executive Committee's members, a community of people united by political ideas should not have numerical restrictions or organizational structure. However, they also believed that a community of people united not only by common ideas but also by joint activities aimed at realizing these ideas was possible. Such a community would be numerically limited and organizationally structured. Alexander Mikhailov, who led «Narodnaya Volya» for several years, wrote about this: «The party is a specific group of like-minded people not bound by any mutual obligations. Organization, in addition to the mandatory condition of unity of thought, implies a certain closedness, close cohesion, and full commitment of relationships. The party includes the organization, but the latter is limited within it. The party is solidarity of thought, while the organization is solidarity of action.»

Volunteers were destined to resort to the path of terrorist struggle because the socio-political system of the Russian Empire did not offer any other solution to the political contradictions of society except violence. The Russian Socialist Revolutionary Party, rejected by conservative masses and constantly suppressed by the imperial government, had no choice but to either leave politics or learn more about Russian political struggle before responding to violence.

Typically, violence becomes an axiom of political struggle when no alternatives are available. A political regime that replaces a legitimate dialogue accepted by both sides (both the government and the opposition) with a system of permanent repressive actions against its opponents sooner or later becomes the target of terrorist influence. Spontaneous and fragmented contractions of terrorist groups relative to representatives of state power, initially impulsive and sporadic, over time transform into a permanently present methodological gestalt, where violence becomes the foundational principle.

Thus, the absence of channelized legal means and methods to resolve political conflicts sooner or later results in the chaos of violent confrontation, where terror and terrorism become fundamental.